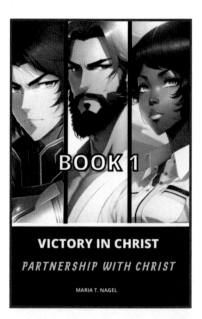

BOOK 1

VICTORY IN CHRIST

PARTNERSHIP WITH CHRIST

MARIA T. NAGEL

COMIC BOOK SERIES

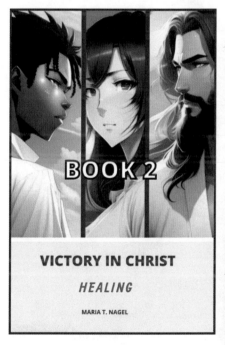

BOOK 2

VICTORY IN CHRIST

HEALING

MARIA T. NAGEL

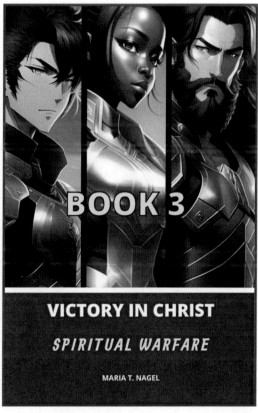

BOOK 3

VICTORY IN CHRIST

SPIRITUAL WARFARE

MARIA T. NAGEL

THE AFRICA & DIASPORA EDITION

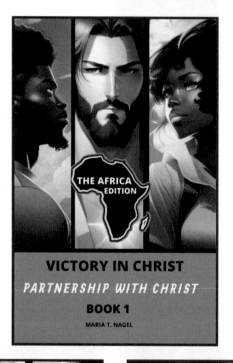

VICTORY IN CHRIST
PARTNERSHIP WITH CHRIST
BOOK 1
MARIA T. NAGEL

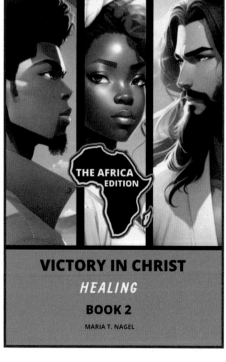

VICTORY IN CHRIST
HEALING
BOOK 2
MARIA T. NAGEL

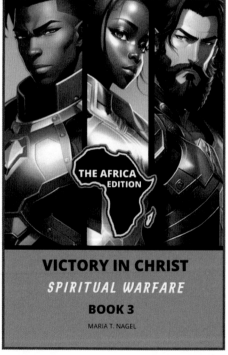

VICTORY IN CHRIST
SPIRITUAL WARFARE
BOOK 3
MARIA T. NAGEL

FOR WOMEN & TEEN GIRLS

SCAN ME

**SCAN THIS QR CODE
FOR DIRECT ACCESS
TO THE AMAZON REVIEW PAGE**

SHARE YOUR EXPERIENCE

Disclaimer

It is crucial to seek assistance from medical or mental health professionals when managing pain to ensure precise diagnosis, effective treatment, and necessary support.

This comic book is not a substitute for medical advice. If you are experiencing pain or have any health concerns, it is strongly advised to consult with a qualified healthcare professional. They can offer personalized guidance tailored to your individual circumstances and assist you in navigating your journey towards pain management.

**WHAT DOES
THE BIBLE SAY
ABOUT HEALING?**

The Bible teaches us that while physical healing may not always occur in the way we desire or expect

God's plans for our lives includes ultimate and complete healing and restoration.

4

In Jesus Christ,
we can find hope,
comfort and
the assurance that God
is present in our pain
and suffering,
offering healing
and wholeness.

The bible teach us that
Jesus Christ is
the ultimate source of healing
and restoration
for our well-being.

5

In Jesus Christ,
we can find hope,
comfort and
the assurance that God
is present in our pain
and suffering,
offering healing
and wholeness.

6

Through a personal relationship with Him,
we can find comfort and strength,
enabling us to navigate the complexities
of pain with resilience and hope.

His teachings of truth, forgiveness,
and the renewal of the mind
offer a path towards mental
and emotional wholeness.

Here are some examples of the types of pain
one can suffer from.

Mike suffers from Emotional Pain:
This type of pain is about psychological
or emotional distress.
It can arise from experiences such as grief,
heartbreak, loneliness, rejection, guilt, or trauma.

Emotional pain can manifest as sadness, anxiety, depression, or a sense of emptiness.

JESUS CHRIST
HEALS

Lin Lin suffers from Social Pain.
Social pain refers to the distress that arises
from negative social interactions
or feelings of exclusion, rejection, or isolation.
It can be caused by bullying, exclusion,
or the breakdown of social relationships.

12

Social pain can lead to feelings of loneliness,
humiliation, or a lack of belonging.

JESUS CHRIST
HEALS

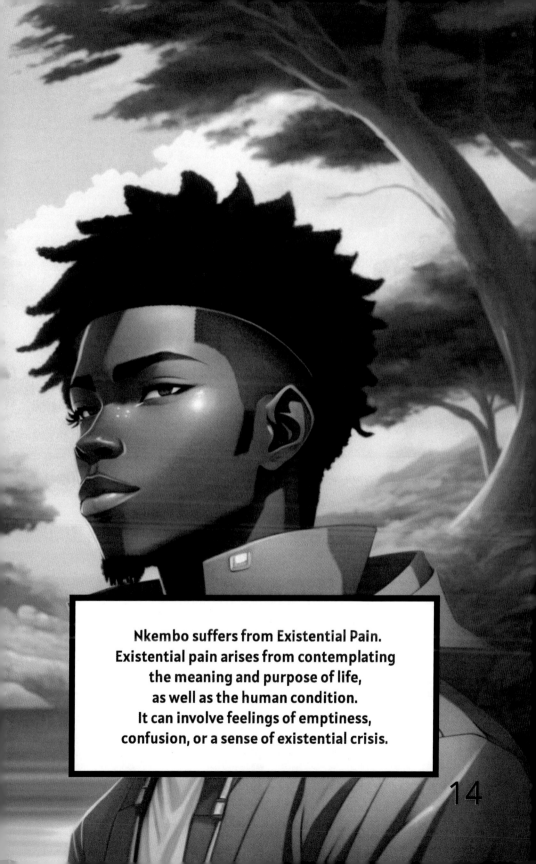

Nkembo suffers from Existential Pain.
Existential pain arises from contemplating
the meaning and purpose of life,
as well as the human condition.
It can involve feelings of emptiness,
confusion, or a sense of existential crisis.

14

Existential pain often arises when individuals have questions about identity, mortality, or the meaning of life.

JESUS CHRIST HEALS

Jennifer suffers from Psychological Pain.
Psychological pain encompasses a wide
range of mental and emotional distress.
It can include conditions such as anxiety disorders,
mood disorders, depression,
post-traumatic stress disorder (PTSD),
and other mental health conditions.

Psychological pain often affects a person's thoughts, emotions, and overall well-being.

JESUS CHRIST HEALS

Habib suffers from Chronic Pain.
Chronic pain is a persistent and long-lasting
physical or psychological pain
that lasts beyond the expected
healing time. It can result from various
conditions such as arthritis, migraines,
or chronic back pain..

18

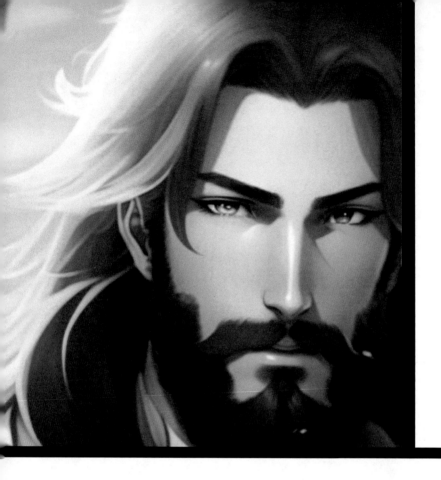

Chronic pain can significantly impact
an individual's daily life and well-being.

JESUS CHRIST
HEALS

Bintu suffers from Spiritual Pain.
Spiritual pain relates to a sense of disconnection
or distress in one's spiritual beliefs
and practices. It can occur when individuals
experience a loss of faith or
conflicts with their beliefs.

20

Spiritual pain can result
in feelings of emptiness,
spiritual crisis, or a loss of purpose.

JESUS CHRIST
SAVES & HEALS

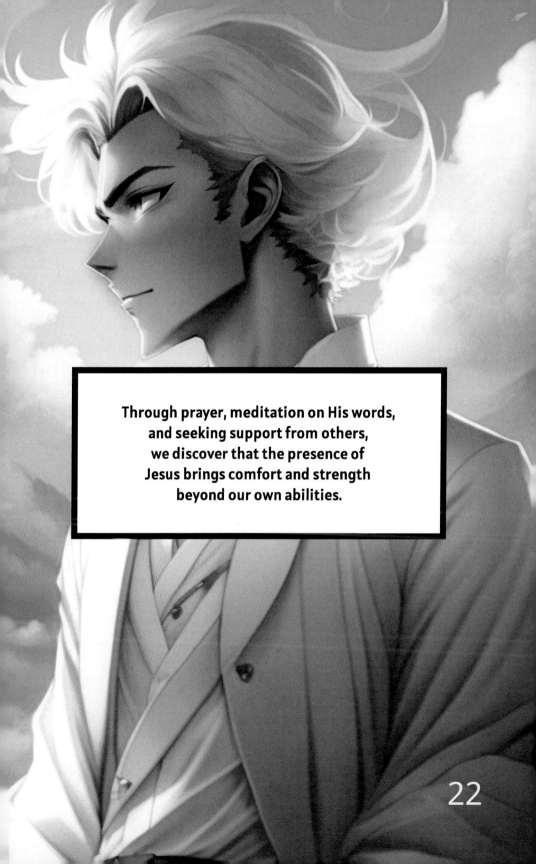

Through prayer, meditation on His words,
and seeking support from others,
we discover that the presence of
Jesus brings comfort and strength
beyond our own abilities.

22

As we navigate the complexities of pain,
we can hold onto the promises found in the bible,
finding assurance in God's love and the transformative
power of faith in Jesus Christ.

23

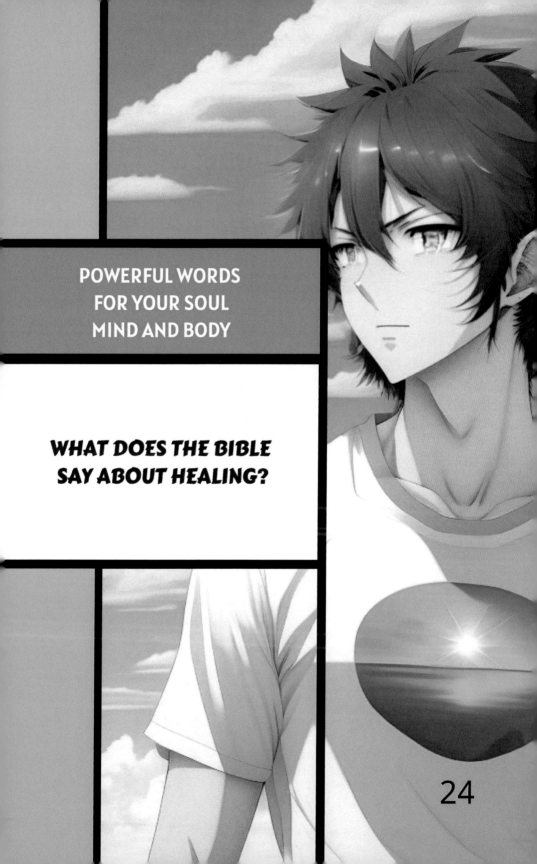

"I know the plans I have for you," says the LORD. "They are plans for good and not for disaster, to give you a future and a hope". Jeremiah 29:11

You must serve only the LORD your God. If you do, I will bless you with food and water. Exodus 23:25

26

I will restore you to health and heal
your wounds, declares the LORD. Jeremiah 30:17

27

He was pierced for our rebellion,
crushed for our sins.
He was beaten
so we could be whole.
He was whipped so we could be healed.
Isaiah 53:5

The Sun of Righteousness will rise
with healing in his wings.
And you will go free, leaping with joy
like calves let out to pasture. Malachi 4:2

JESUS CHRIST
SAVES & HEALS

30

You are my hiding place; you will protect me
from trouble and surround
me with songs of deliverance. Psalm 32:7

31

Don't be afraid, for I am with you. Don't be discouraged,
for I am your God. I will strengthen you and help you.
I will hold you up with my victorious
right hand.Isaiah 41:10

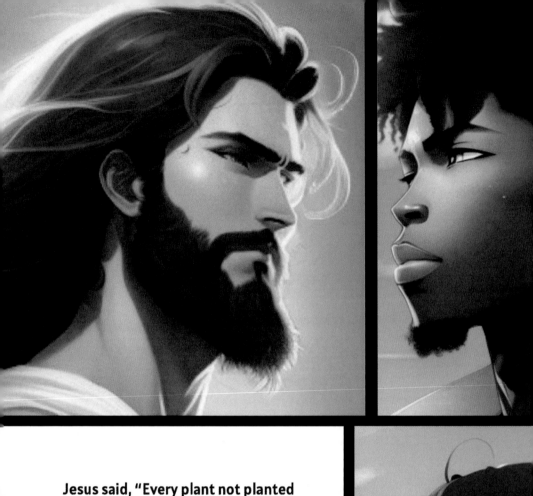

Jesus said, "Every plant not planted
by my heavenly Father
will be uprooted". Matthew 15:13

33

Don't be afraid, for I am with you.
Don't be discouraged,
for I am your God.
I will strengthen you and help you.
I will hold you up with my victorious right hand.
Isaiah 41:10

Dear friend, I hope all is well with you
and that you are as healthy
in body as you are strong in spirit. 3 John 1:2

35

Peace I leave with you;
my peace I give you.
I do not give to you
as the world gives.
Do not let your hearts
be troubled and
do not be afraid. John 14:27

Take my yoke upon you, and learn from me,
for I am gentle and lowly in heart,
and you will find rest for your souls.
Matthew 11:29

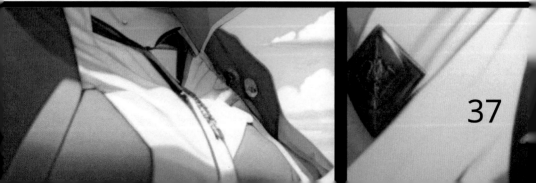

37

I consider that our present sufferings are not worth
comparing with the glory that will be revealed in us.
Romans 8:18

39

And my God will meet all
your needs
according to the riches
of his glory in Christ Jesus.
Philippians 4:19

Jesus heals.

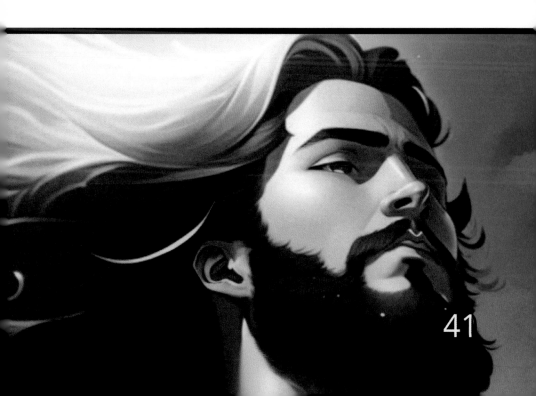

The Lord is close to the brokenhearted
and saves those
who are crushed in spirit. Psalm 34:18

Be kind and compassionate to one another,
forgiving each other,
just as in Christ God forgave you. Ephesians 4:32

43

We do not lose heart. Though outwardly
we are wasting away,
yet inwardly we are being renewed day by day.
For our light and momentary troubles are achieving
for us an eternal glory
that far outweighs them all.
So we fix our eyes not on what is seen,
but on what is unseen since
what is seen is temporary,
but what is unseen is eternal. 2 Corinthians 4:16-18

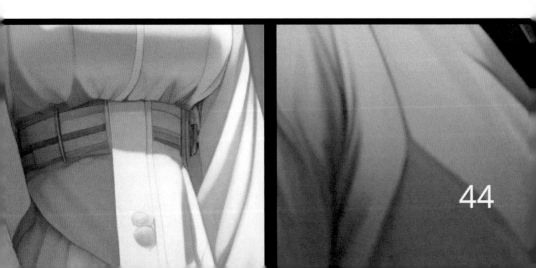

Love your enemies,
do good to those who hate you,
bless those who curse you,
pray for those who mistreat you.
Luke 6:27-28

45

Love your enemies, do good
to those who hate you,
bless those who curse you, pray for those
who mistreat you. Luke 6:27-28

46

Do not be anxious about anything,
but in every situation,
by prayer and petition,
with thanksgiving, present
your requests to God.
And the peace of God, which transcends
all understanding,
will guard your hearts
and your minds in Christ Jesus.
Philippians 4:6-7

Behold, I will bring to it health and healing,
and I will heal them and reveal to them
abundance of prosperity and security. Jeremiah 33:6

A joyful heart is good medicine,
but a crushed spirit dries up the bones.
Proverbs 17:22

49

Come to me, all you who are weary
and burdened, and I will give you rest. Matthew 11:28

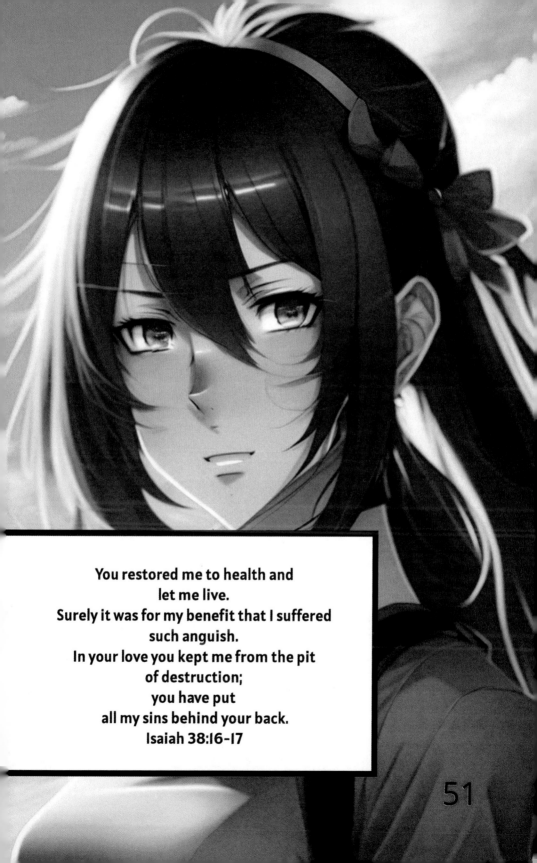

You restored me to health and
let me live.
Surely it was for my benefit that I suffered
such anguish.
In your love you kept me from the pit
of destruction;
you have put
all my sins behind your back.
Isaiah 38:16-17

Nevertheless, I will bring health and healing to it;
I will heal my people and
will let them enjoy abundant peace and security.
Jeremiah 33:6

The Lord sustains him on his sickbed;
in his illness you restore him to full health. Psalm 41:3

Thank you Jesus.

Nevertheless, I will bring health
and healing to it;
I will heal my people and will let them enjoy
abundant peace and security.
Jeremiah 33:6

55

He will wipe every tear from their eyes.
There will be no more death' or mourning or
crying or pain, for the old order of things has passed away.
Revelations 21:4

My son, pay attention to what I say;
turn your ear to my words.
Do not let them out of your sight,
keep them within your heart;
for they are life to those who find them
and health to one's whole body.
Proverbs 4:20-22

Then they cried to the LORD in their trouble,
and he saved them
from their distress.
He sent out his word and healed them;
he rescued them from the grave.
Let them give thanks to the LORD
for his unfailing love and his wonderful
deeds for mankind. Psalms 107:19-21

Praise the LORD, my soul, and forget
not all his benefits
who forgives all your sins and heals
all your diseases,
who redeems your life from the pit
and crowns you with
love and compassion. Psalms 103:2-4

LORD my God, I called to you for help,
and you healed me. Psalms 30:2

60

He gives strength to the weary and
increases the power of the weak. Isaiah 40:29

Hear, LORD, and be merciful to me; LORD, be my help.
You turned my wailing into dancing;
you removed my sackcloth and clothed me with joy.
Psalms 30:10-11

He heals the brokenhearted and bandages
their wounds.Psalm 147:3

Made in the USA
Monee, IL
13 December 2024

73714410R00040